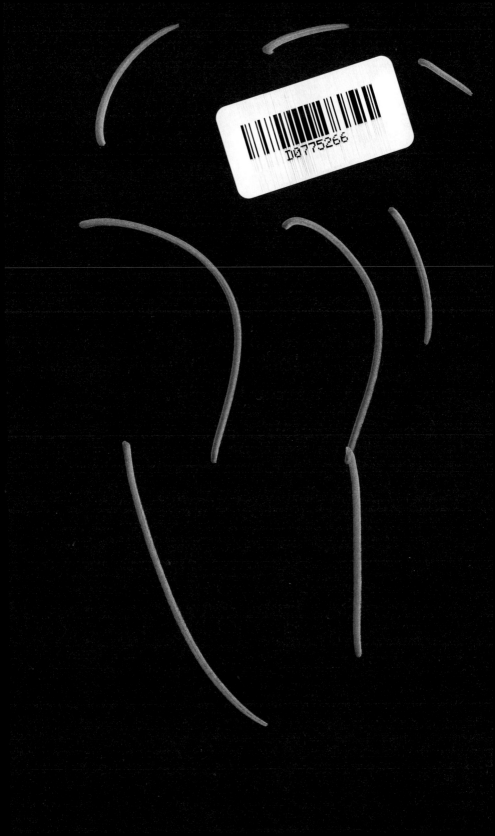

Grief Notes & Animal Dreams

Grief Notes & Animal Dreams

Jane Southwell Munro

*for Keith
with many thanks
for inviting me
to Malaspina —
good writers in
your 8 months!
Jane*

Brick Books

CANADIAN CATALOGUING IN PUBLICATION DATA

Munro, Jane, 1943-
  Grief notes & animal dreams

Poems.
ISBN 0-919626-82-3

I. Title. II. Title: Grief notes and animal dreams.

PS8576.U574G75 1995   C811'.54   C95-932305-8
PR9199.3.M85G75 1995

The support of the Canada Council and the Ontario Arts Council is gratefully acknowledged. The support of the Government of Ontario through the Ministry of Culture, Tourism and Recreation is also gratefully acknowledged.

Cover is after a character, Li (The Clinging, Fire), from the Chinese *Book of Changes* or *I Ching*.

Typeset in Trump Mediaeval. Printed and bound by The Porcupine's Quill. The stock is acid-free Zephyr Antique laid.

Brick Books
431 Boler Road, Box 20081
London, Ontario
N6K 4G6

for Bob

and in memory of my parents

Evelyn Elizabeth Southwell
&
Charles Raymond Southwell

Contents

'Tis not the swaying frame we miss,
It is the steadfast Heart

Emily Dickinson, #1597 c.1884

Grief Notes & Animal Dreams

The fire the packrat started
destroyed the house my father built
and killed my mother.
Its aftermath sits in me like a drought.

And I, a forest creature, grown
among mists, between creek beds,
where, if water evaporates
it's only for a few hours
of rest in another state
as if to catch a little sleep,
before falling again –
I keep expecting the drought to end.

It's as if grief
sucked the green world inside out,
down through its roots
into a closed and cryptic seed,
ran gratitude backwards
like a movie rewinding.

Now, in my dream, the treeless hills are arid
and below the cellar
under the house
the earth is tunneled, as if a mine started there,
and out of the passage
parched animals emerge.
First a deer, terribly close to death.

Upstairs, a little water spills
through the cracks, floor to floor
when the family washes dishes
and I see a silver rivulet
bead and twist as it slips between the planks,
but the air in the cellar vacuums it up.

The animals from underground come
with tongues white and crystallized
like pieces of Turkish delight.

Despite the drought
I find a working garden hose, the alligator kind
mother went after
when she, safely outside,
remembering water in the greenhouse off father's bedroom,
ran back inside.
The kind of hose clearly in her mind when the inferno
filled the hall
and she crawled along the floor beneath ten feet of flame
that tore the skin from her back
devoured the flesh off her feet,
a fire so hot it crumbled slabs of granite six inches thick,
melted brass, left her with third degree burns
to more than fifty percent of her body.
I hold a running garden hose
in the cellar
and a silvery-eyed doe
leaning against the hard-packed dirt tunnel
lets me fill her mouth
but she can't swallow.

In my dream I taste the brine
dissolving round her tongue,
so absolutely stiff with salt
the first water that hits it turns caustic.

And it takes a minute
because the drought and the dream slow my mind
before I realize she need not swallow it:
I have in my hands a running hose
though outside the hillside is brown and treeless,
and I don't know where the water comes from.
I am able to rinse her mouth again
and again, if need be, until it softens
and she can swallow.

Wanting

Talking to the ghost of desire
I asked him
why he'd moved his rehearsal hall,
his stirring of the air before his orchestra,
his exuberant timing, his encouragements,
far, far away.
Talking to him as I walked was like praying
or attending
to static behind music on the radio.

Though partly I was yelling at myself: numbskull!
Trudging across campus through the snow,
furious with myself for wanting,
spitting damn mad at that trap,
kicking my loneliness so it remembered
what hurt felt like,
marking the past in a neat diagonal
of feet pointing towards maturity ....

I dreamt of an aunt who died five years ago:
she was upstairs holding court
over breakfast in an English hotel.
Her body, respirited, recognized me.
She crumpled, saying my name – *Jane* –

and I heard anguish, surprise, welcome, exhaustion
voiced in that chord of longing.
As if she'd counted on my presence for days,
perhaps years, but I hadn't arrived.
As if my opening the door on her audience
were gauche, as if it destroyed thought, destroyed her
but restored hope.

The way she called my name! I flooded into that word
even though she was dead and in a wheelchair.
Her hotel was full
and many meals and conversations had taken place
without me. What was I doing

stamping through a glittering winter,
hankering after desire?
I didn't need to want like this.
I didn't want to want so much
– only, to swim into perfection freely.

Romance

Falling in love with him pulled me
out of myself like pulling a wet hand

out of a leaking rubber glove.
I would say it had nothing to do with him –

the glove fell away from my grasp, inside out.
He seized upon a woman I hadn't allowed myself to be.

A snake drops its former cover, crumpled skin.
I'd say it wasn't him I needed, but me.

A snake splits when it's ready, naturally.
Falling in love with him did what seeing mystic lights,

listening to good advice, reading novels
hadn't accomplished. That wildness.

Of course it had to do with him. We flew
out of wet gloves, bare hands gesturing.

Do you know D'Sonoqua's mask, Old Woman of the Woods?
Falling in love, I paid tribute to a cannibal spirit.

Little piles of gloves: marigold, pink, yellow
in the woods below her white face, her mouth like an O.

Helicopter By The Lake

Its blades turn invisible,
but their chop
has destroyed the membrane
in which she'd closed his voice.
His drumming in her thoughts
is gone, though little pulses of his intonations
still peak and fall through her skin.
The air oscillates
between her and the metal dragonfly.
Pentecostal, a wordless conversational uproar
transports her attention.
The lake's batiked crinkle
crumples with waves.

Waves from the rotor, waves from the wind,
waves from the moon and sun and passing boats
subside. Still, there's no silence.
Not that she's listening for silence.
She's trying to hear the future, and thinks silence
might help, but what she keeps listening to is him.
His eyes close; hers stay open.
A man's purr as he almost snores,
her ear on his clavicle.

He never finished his story
– it disintegrated in the event –
suggesting accident, perhaps a precedent.
A glinting little worry she lets wing away
as the helicopter darts across the lake.
No whirlwind lifted her from the grassy shore
– chances are, she won't fly over the rainbow –
and indeed, she can no longer sense the engine's roar.

Wood Box

If time is a local muscle
bound to the bone it moves ....
If time bears itself, as a zygote does a baby ....
If time curls round us like the jet stream, circulating
atoms of oxygen in and out of bodies ....

I wouldn't ask
except I dreamt of fire – dreamt twice
not on the flat screen of my darkened mind,
I dreamt of fire in virtual reality – dreamt
then woke, and still the dream went on.

Fire drifted,
fingered things, claimed this and that.
Ran along beams, scrambled up logs.
Then, convinced, drove a root through the floor.
Burst, amaryllis, above the roof.

Smoke like a wool rug about my shoulders.
Choked, sitting upright, eyes open –
staring at floating petals of flame –
Father! the cry I tried to make.

When the dream left me in my own home,
in a body I could move,
room to room, I checked on sleeping children.

Five months earlier
the first blaze sprinted across the drapes.
I stumbled to the window, shook the pleats,
then waking further, saw
only moonlight spattered on the walls.

Did I know? Foresee
the fire in my parents' home? My mother's death?

The oldest brain projects a web
then sways in the middle of her trap.
Out-foxing logic, our dream-maker
winds a silver screen limb to limb
and catches the fog of a dripping forest.

Surely the house fire was not time's arson ....
And my mother's action –
her plunge into the burning house to grab a hose –
sprang true: her free, predictable, response ....

Ashes. Ashes in my hand.
Fire terrifies me –
for myself, for my family.
Maybe love is coal or oil or gas
and I am wood,
laid between others, in a wooden box.

Extended Care

Her mouth a multifold difficulty.
Out of body. Can she find herself in this shabby purse?
She thought she'd pocketed her navel.

The smelly, urinous, startled old.

Wanting to remember
the underarm stretch of bush down a hill.

I tuck her into a wheelchair,
pick up pieces of thought
from spilled trunks of vocabulary.

From under her drooping eyelid
comes the gaze of a girl.
Despite aphasia,
she cries – *Mother!*

Which woman
would grow decrepit on purpose?

Agitation:
a crow, gripped by its legs.
Black wings flap across my field of vision.

Her denim smock,
its pockets of brushes.
At six, sitting in a blue dress for her. That portrait burned
in the house fire that killed my mother.
My aunt, sending me a tambourine,
a buckskin jacket with fringes.

The smell, the smell and
tears coming down in the elevator,
plucking leaves off the bushes outside,
pulling them apart.

Terminal

Look, she departed from a castle of a place:
Victoria Station, Charing Cross, Place de Ville,
Le Gare de L'Est, or Kushadashi – those steel, glass
and tiled terminals with their migrant
flocks of steam and sparks, migrant storms
of voices, and their strident slide
of steel wheels on rails. She left
world capitals with opera houses and art galleries,
Copenhagen, Vienna, Madrid, Rome – look,
without a timetable, without a guide, without
passport, destination or companion.

Animal Lives

Near a reef off a northern island,
a grey and white seal pup
churned up to our rowboat, bleating constantly,
dove under the hull, surfaced by an oar.
We could see it plainly. It had no visible injury
but it was alone.

I wanted to scoop the baby up,
rock it against my stomach, make promises:
– *it's ok, it's ok.*
After a while the orphan left, crying and thrashing,
and we rowed away.

In Vancouver my lonely father
(missing his wife, three brothers, two sisters, both parents)
bobs around the widows –
Helen, Hilda, Barbara, Marge, Leslie –
drifts like a jellyfish bereft of tentacles.
Stars with crusty arms, the widows
reach and release, cram themselves together –
orange, pink, purple – in a dark crease of rockface.

Back east, my friend is dying.
Mail accumulates, a sediment of paper hopes,
in the drawer of her bedside table,
and on the window sill.
Outside, poplars about the yard
toss wind hand to hand without dropping it.
The house shimmers with pain
becoming visible to people in airplanes.

While we waited for the ferry
a seagull fell from the sky over Nanaimo,
dropped dead in mid-flight, crashed on the road –
feet up, long tail feathers twisted to one side.
After a while a young woman walked over,
squatted, studied the gull,
tested its feet with her hand,
then dragged the corpse out of the way.

Entering death, numbers disappear.
How many lives pass in a moment?
Earth, in its luminous fruit of water and air,
sheds more and more animal flesh from its core.

Dream: Housing The Seam

She smiles towards us through the window.
Or, perhaps, she smiles at someone behind us.
We have waited for her on a granite outcrop.
She has come to us, bringing her childhood home.

Hers is quite a window: two large plates of glass
touch at right angles, no post between them.
My father, the engineer, once dug his penknife
into the cedar sill of such a window.
Wet. Punk. You see, he said, *the view's great,*
but glass expands and contracts. You need
to house the seam.

We have been outside all afternoon.
First, we climbed the hill: stunted bushes
lodged in fissures between rough domes of stone.
A crowd assembled. Then she arrived
and led us down the far side to the house.
It's sort of a museum about her, in this park.

I bought, then lost, a postcard
of the place. Reminds me of an architect's retreat.
Hand-built home. The roof an angled wing,
as if a huge hawk reached out to cover her
and her family while she grew up.
Weathered shingles almost soft.

Behind the window she wears a sweater.
I guess her smile was for someone else.
It hurts to look at the unmarked corner
where two panes butt, one against the other.
At their imperfect seam.
Which does allow us to see past her,
through her bedroom, across the hill,
into the trees.

Even With All Our Windows

we shall only catch glimpses of the real world
— A.S. Byatt, *Still Life*

We are playing bride on the sidewalk.
It's a bossy game and I'm the littlest.
Wrapped in a white curtain,
I hold a dandelion bouquet.
One of the big girls yells at me, yanks
milky stems from my fist,
shoves me out of the procession.

Unwinding yard goods
I escape across an empty lot.
Broken glass sticks up from raw mud.
It takes quick twists
not to get cut.
Mother's ironing in the kitchen.
If she sees me she'll bang on the window.
If I ignore her and keep running,
I'll get a spanking.

The back side of the house next door
is tar-papered. That woman smokes
while she hangs out the laundry. Mother
edges away from talking with her.
Sheets flap on the clothes-lines. I'm out
on the streets in my slip

because I hate their dumb game. The big girls
play it day after day. Out front, parading.
Twenty houses, twenty wives on the block.
I can see each mother, thick or thin,
set in her gesture of wanting.
My mind clicks across them
like a stick hitting a line of pickets.

Cottontail

He nosed the car around the corner. It drifted noisily
onto gravel. One foot slowly depressed the clutch.
There were no windows looking out on you here.
Only second-growth forest and blackberries.

The bushes hid a sign:
No Hunting. No Trespassing.
He had never done this before, nothing like this,
stopping the way a man might who was nursing an idea
about you. This man you'd known for years, who was just
giving you a ride home, turned off the ignition.
When the motor quit shuddering you felt his fingers
trace the contour of your ear, touch your neck.
You stared straight ahead. The sign was the sort
sold in hardware stores. You gripped your purchase.
He didn't explain. His hand dropped. Its weight
through your coat. Friend. Giving you a lift.

Without parting, the two of you sat very still,
you holding the milk carton and he your shoulder,
accepting and refusing, exactly
what the situation called for.

Nursery Rhyme

She could plant a furious camellia
to shout in spring's procession

and a magnolia
to finger light through petals
teased from calyxes of mouse fur.

She could dig bulbs down in October:
tiger lilies to recall
diatribes from country ditches,
daffodils, tulips – also rhizomes,
for iris trumpet flesh.

She could stay there, outside Eden,
outside logic, and plant corollas of outrage,
reinventing promise with flowers.
She could flaunt them round her house
raw as skinned dreams.

Queen Anne's Lace

Raindrops lengthen as slowly as fingernails
to claw out chambers in a thunderhead.
Slubs of hail
white as bees' or ants' eggs
hatch grubs of water
when they fall. Summer after summer
they've hived bedrock
until its crystals crumble
like dropped insect wings.

Up Desolation Sound, extinct blue volcanoes
promise death will come again.
On an island in their rain-shadow
it's washday. Her laces and linen
are laid out to bleach and tighten.

Lust races into brittle thickets,
fires the mantles
of manzanita blooms.

Tread carefully
down this dark slope
for the queen's Monday bodices
are foaming, pungent as herbs,
wanton as the thorn bushes
on which her pretties hang
while she is outrunning her weeds.

Night Tiger

His stripes simply won't stay put. They detach,
rippling on the air's current, permitting
risk to permeate the dining room.
If he were not clearly a tiger
she'd swear he was a man, one elbow on the table
twisting a glass of dark wine.

Without her permission
the tiger has taken charge
and begun his dream of a woman.

She persists
in a kind of politeness, obliquely
trying to preside over him, the meal
and some pretty children.
A spoon for the cream! Child, you may be excused.
Wainscoting boxes the room at their backs.
The stained walnut reeks
with contained smoke. Wary, she changes her face
and that is enough to gentle his approach.
Evening inhales; she proposes: *Bring your port –*
let us continue in the living room,
then stands purposefully, shedding felted air.

Her proper guests wait
like fixtures in the next room –
these unknown friends she must have fed.
A dress, in fact a gown, slides on her thighs.
She notices its drape from her bosom.
So, this was long ago, this conjunction.
She is allowed Edwardian skin for it
and milk-breasts. She is allowed
a needle-point settee and another man
whose eyes doze behind fronds of twilight.
A man asleep in a wool suit,
like a northern lake. She is allowed
to rest on his surface, break her flight
for a few sips of coffee.

The tiger enters to brood over his hostess.
She lifts away, flushed from the unsuitable couch,
tries the door. The wake of her party
rises after her. Pushed from behind,
she bursts onto the patio, but the others
can't fit through the shrinking frame.

The tiger is already outside. She senses
there's been some preparation
she overlooked, a menu for the night
which might explain why she's followed him.
While the woman combs his dream, the tiger,
with his rough tongue, licks clean the starry sky.
It remains unaccountable
this wish she has to lean
full-length against him
enfolded in his tresses, his risky stripes,
rising past the houses of the zodiac.

Festina Lente

We circle Stanley Park,
two women moving briskly as we talk.
You deserve a good man as much as anyone,
she says, tossing an arm across my wet shoulders.
It's raining, true Vancouver.
The heron by Siwash Rock is huge,
his feathers drooping in tendrils.

The tide has flicked gravel across the path.
Below the walkway, reclining bodies of waves
do leglifts over boulders.
The sea is too full for its dark bowl:

active. Tonight I need to sleep.
Sleep is a large park, circled
by this sea wall, round which we trudge,
talking of a summer that hasn't happened yet.

Will it ever be enough
to love the herons
who now and then heave themselves
into deliberate flight?

Moving Too Fast

I carry an empty heart
like a loose backpack
slung from one shoulder,
the bottom of it littered
with pens, tampons, TO DO lists,
but it is really empty.

I heard on the CBC
some rats are genetically sociable
– an impressive group –
but the most ardent lovers
are born loners who've been given attention.

*

Last night, drinking Campari and eating cheese
after he, in his agitated head of lists,
pulled his shorts on, left.
One hour. Another item.
I'm damned if I'll be had like this, just damned.
Grieving all day – broccoli, eggs, cantaloupe,
bagels overflowing the terraces of hell.

*

Running five miles tonight
alone along the beaches: slip-stitching
shade trees, hummocks of lawn,
sand pits where my ankles turn,
tall grass full of hoppers,
broken glass, empty chip bags,
the yard of masts clinking in the breeze,
trim figures in wet suits lugging wind
surfers across the parking lot.
Running slowly for the first mile
but ending loose – hips free –
strides long, fast: I could run
to the Planetarium without feeling it, run
to False Creek, past Granville Island.

Run to keep my feet on the ground.

Rolling Over The World At Night

ten days away
pink roses by my bed will shed
perfume and petals
I'll inhale another place
exhale his touch

ten days away
two bare stems will stick
out of the green vase
and skirting its base
close to a hundred sleeping hands

What I've Left

Is a man's bed with pink sheets,
messy, musty-smelling forest,
damp nostrils, slugs
at the end of glistening tracks,
stuck to the sidewalk in the morning
when I open the door for the paper.
Is a room without curtains
at midnight – is canyons, fjords –
the impossibility of lodging
permanently in loneliness.

Not Sterling

Pewter water left for ten days
to clarify in the Maytag washer
won't solve its broken pump.
I'll return, call for service, spend
a lot of money. Solid fact
stuck in the future.

Pewter water in the harbour, pewter sky
predict a July storm in Vancouver.
Normal problems return.
You look smashing, she says.
I feel surprised.
Pewter slugs ate the cabbage.
Pewter salt and pepper shakers
sit on the table like stubby little pricks.

Thinking #1

As two deer
our minds graze.

Knowing is a grazing.
It is mealy salal berries.

It is the blue stain on her two cheeks.

At age two, she sat
on the sod over the septic tank, to look
across the street curved
like the edge of an open eyelid.

Knowing is a crescent below her
of uncurtained houses with vinyl siding,
each centred in its lot.

As deer do
mind startles
when the child stands
and touches our hides.
Mind steps out of view.

Two deer wade uphill.
Hooves skid on granite, sink
one after the other, into moss
under eyelashes of forest.

We graze as an onshore breeze grazes.

Thinking is the eight feet
of the two of us
wading a waterfall of salal
above the duroid roofs of a western suburb.

Did it occur that the thought
of us grazing is only a dreaming?
Deer knowing thought move,
sift through dozing.

Thinking is the blue-eyed gaze
of a daughter, mid-morning,
her fists full. She picks
a rhythm for grazing uphill.

Thinking #2

This concept of dog:
a section of rainbow near the sun.
The sun-dog warns of snow
and worries a farmer.

This concept of farm:
domed turrets of a castle,
all aluminium, cement, limestone.
Its trickle of Holsteins
frozen in a contour of the hill.
Wheels of cheddar roll from its cellar.
The farm a fortress in a county criss-crossed
with roads. The cows monitored by computers.

This concept of cemetery:
congregation of chalky monuments
bleached as pale as corn husks
in mid-November fields. Patrons,
leaving the stadium, game over.
The old slabs stand, tilted, the height
of emergent teenagers.

The dog, for Diogenes, was swift
empirical thought, carrying all things with him.
Dogs of the spirit world grin
at the gate of Tibetan temples.
Fire dogs guard a burning log.
The dog star is fixed and bright.
Dogs of war hunt without knowing mercy.

Where I come from, a dog is a grey shark,
the fish without scales who grabs at lines
and snaps them. Time is the hunger
that folds things neatly in its chest of fog.
Death rides on the branches of cedar in boxes of cedar
crested with frogs or bears. The land
streams through a farm like thoughts through
one mind. A prismatic arrangement of earth-dogs
pads through the landscape, warning
of ice-age, warning of those
flows of lava, rock, glacier, ocean
into whose contours we crowd this winter morning.

Dream: Emptying The Premises

School is out. Students
accumulate along the curb.
You leave with your first load of books,
pick a twisting route down the stairs
to sidestep lounging couples.

Returning to an empty classroom
you clear away crumbs of a cherry cake,
collect sticky, scattered paper plates.
The demolition crew arrives next week.

A fat woman in the scullery
has done the washing-up.
Others mill about, open cupboards,
pack boxes. You pick up a pot of dirt,
ask the dishwasher, *does this go too?*
The woman with wet hands rises to tip-toe, taken
with admiration for the possible
swedish ivy, geranium, philodendron.
Her imagination dances. She's aglow.

Finally, you leave empty-handed.
The year has turned on itself
like folded gloves.
From here, summer looks like a shelf.

Li – The Clinging, Fire

Grief is a scree slope
high in the Rockies.
When I sit in the sunshine a chipmunk
runs up my sock.
See how I avoid the truth?
My father is collapsing.
I cling
to him, and the contours he has lost. The mountain
slips from itself.
Roped together, we continue our climb.
Broken rock
rattles as it plunges. A cloud nests
in the chimney above us.
There is no easy route ahead
and afterwards, I will have to come down.
He told me, *Pick your descent*
while you're going up, so you don't get stuck.
I don't know when his legs will give out.
The top of the mountain
is no place to pitch a tent,
but we have packed survival gear
and could possibly huddle
in the full blast of the wind,
clinging to the view and each other.
A valley with its turquoise lake
eyes us from far, far below.
We can't take much of a rest.
Daylight tips higher up the slope
and he is determined to stay
within it. Each breath burns
more of his irreplaceable strength.

Candy

Full moon between skyscrapers
like a nougat centre
waiting to be dipped in bitter chocolate.
Downtown castles, storefront chapels of joy,
beauty shops, cheque cashing joints,
wine & beer, and furniture paid for next year.
Cars chilled and shiny. And underground,
in parking lots, alarms bark.

Up three dark flights, the apartment's
wooden floor rolls under peasant rugs.
Bathroom thick with orange paint.
Bowl of daisies. Bach on a harpsichord.
Old church pew and canvas butterfly-wing chair.
Three deadbolts on the turquoise door.

In the kitchen, a boy steals cooking chocolate
– unsweetened blocks from the top shelf –
refolds the wrappers into empty cubes, tucks
the white papers back into the box,
hopes his mother won't notice.

She discovers the little deceit
when she goes to bake his birthday cake.
His sly greed bewilders her.
If he thought he wasn't stealing,
why refold the wrappers? He'll get fat.

Down at the corner a girl
waits, walkman in her pocket,
red line to her ear.
Back of her, the tennis courts
are filled with tents made of garbage bags.
A man in an unraveled sweater limps
across the park. Another writhes
on brownstone steps, snaps to his fellow,
I know what I done. Heroin's a bitch.
Subway signs offer prayer on an 800-line.

Our craving for salvation is a white paper
refolded, tucked in its blue box.
Love, packaged as a pleasure,
tastes false when it comes unsugared.
But what's to be done, in the aftermath of romance?
Wards of need,
our candy wrappers in every gutter.

Towards A Researchable Question: It Must Be Testable

A fence rotted at its foot:
severed boards flop in a sleeve of vines.

A man is held up by veins.

My death is held up by veins.

Weeping over the onion
in which nest perceptions within concepts within
beliefs within attitudes within values.
Slicing intellectual history across its root.

Do you not believe
we are held up by veins?
Can you see
a shuddering fence
coated with Virginia Creeper?

Towards A Researchable Question: It Must Be Significant: Fanny Bay Bill

Audrey wrote a fiction about living on an island. Bill, who used to have a ponytail and prefers books about fungus or bathhouses, read Audrey's novel. He said it was the best description of island hippie life he'd seen. *I know six of her characters*, he allowed. There is a difference between relevance and significance, but it's sometimes hard to tell. When you share a conceptual framework, detail fascinates and vehicles need only go. Odd trucks run along local roads.

There are several stories about how Fanny Bay got its name. Carol, who lives with Bill, claims the reference is to one of Thomas Hardy's characters, but when I looked her up, she was called Fanny Day. Others say a sailor admired a girl squatting on the sand shucking clams and named the place in his log after her memorable ass. Others outline the peninsula on a map and suggest it resembles a gluteal grin. How significance is found tells first about the mind doing the finding. Second, it suggests context or precedent. Third, but only obliquely, it reflects upon the object named.

Fanny Bay Bill has a rule: leave things better than you found them. He left two fridges full of labeled microcondia; his dissertation was on molds.

Towards A Researchable Question: It Must Be Parsimonious

> *Westron wind, when wilt thou blow?*
> *The small rain down can rain.*
> *Christ, that my love were in my arms,*
> *And I in my bed again.*
> *– Anon*

From the middle ages: a seafarer
becalmed in a downpour,
swore
simply
beseeching cause or force for an effect.
Not mentioning any facts on board,
he repeated
rain
and said what he wanted.

I can see him
as if on TV,
shoulders soaked,
hands chapped,
wet cloth stuck to his ankles.

Law of parsimony: the logical principle that no more causes or
forces should be assumed than are necessary to account for
the facts.
OED

The assumption of Christ
didn't suffice.
Only the wind
– his intimate, thou Westron wind –
would, of its own volition, blow
him home. I can see her in his arms,
her weight on the sheets.

Becalmed, he left room in his prayer
for reiteration.
A little doubling of the account.
Rain. A downfall. He swore
– Christ, if my love –
just in case, as insurance,
for who can say absolutely
about cause or force?

The charm of parsimony:
a nugget lingers,
despite
the slop
of memory. Every theory deserves
sparing expression.

My poem
is not enough
silent.

Towards A Researchable Question: It Must Be Manageable

I dream I am naked and seated
on a wooden floor, surrounded
by babies and toddlers.
I dream I attempt to dress myself
and, simultaneously, prepare a meal.
I dream a man with a chain saw jumps
from the bleachers to the gym floor.
I dream he traps my chest, then rests
his chain of steel thorns across my breast.
Dreaming he means to pull the cord,
start the roar, slice me.
I twist. The bar of his saw strikes my spine,
its line nicks my hip as I fluster away
to hurry preparation
of this crazy meal that refuses realization.
People arrive and collect unfed babies.
I give up hope of clothing.
The teeth of his deadline abrade, avulse
as I work faster.

Remembrance Day

Pulling the cuff of one sock back
across my hand, tucking the toes
of a pair inside one neat sausage.
Pull it open. Presto.

Peripheral, the foil of lightning.

in a drift/dream/mind turns on
itself/pas-de-deux across a dark stage
choreography for the shadow of a mother
apart/folded/floored/legs
and torsos/flex/contract/open/lift
in and out of another body
two-and-one/two/one/two/one-and

The shining of leaves turned underside up.

Puppets on sticks from Rajasthan,
the Maharaja under the woman's skirt.
Her spine an axis between ruler and subject,
male and female, child and crone.
My dream flip-flopping, its costume
covering the head not speaking.
How close to death is the unconscious?

below throat/below chest/out of belly
bass chords/lowing of livestock/snoring/a growl
song like the voice heard through wombwall
Gyuto Tantric Choir/in a drift/dream/mind turns on
Tibetan monks chanting twenty hours a day
one-and-two-and-one/two/one/two/one-and-two-and-one
their vibrations unrattle me

More leaves shaken purple across the wet lawn.

Waking on Remembrance Day to thunder
and blood on the sheets. Thank God it's a holiday.
An old hand at tidying myself.
Pulled together. Pad-lined panty under jeans. Socks.

I saw the lightning while brushing my teeth.

The life and death of the mind.
At times I pick up the phone and expect her voice.
Open and close. Our laundry dances
in drawers, under covers, in washers and dryers
the tumble and turn. How many
thoughts have you folded, shaken out, worn?

mind settles
to tone of stone, the slow pace of bone
in a drift/dream/mind turns on
one-and-two-and-one/two/one-and-two-and-one

Another mind closed in a cuff of thought?

Vibration. Chants to soothe memory
loose in the skeleton.
Turn the flying apart in.

Ashen Flakes

delphiniums
are shadows in the white ice
of mist covering her garden

the lost kitchen full
of dark blossoms, fossilized like Pompeii

how I'd like to shudder out
of this disaster, eat fruit

The Earth Beneath

the lawn
washed away
as if by a river in the night
which bit and gouged
its course down the street
scooping caverns
part of the red cement walk
became a bridge
the front yard
emptied
of its inner substance
only a green rug
and path of concrete
covering the new caves

I reflect on the large
willingness of the faithful, wonder
at the fools of God
– Elijah Harper
and the kids who neighbour me
with their soft, solemn cheeks
– sturdy people
waiting on the shaky grass

I say to them
we must fix this
but there is no extra earth
to fill in the holes
I climb down
look up at the turf roof
stand in that pit
with my hands on my hips

Grandmother Spider Said To Set Aside The Ego Roles

Meaning, I guess, the eighty-two students whose names I knew that semester, and the kitchen crew who were coming for dinner, but especially meaning my dissertation with its false labour pains, occasional spotting, threat of miscarriage. Do something different, she said. Nothing that's a duty. Set an unfamiliar part of your psyche on an unfamiliar path.

I went alone to a warehouse where wool fashions are sewn and I bought, at less than cost: grey trousers, a grey skirt, a matching short grey coat, a green blouse, a patterned pink and grey blouse. I undressed before other women because there were no changing rooms, untying and tying my shoe laces because I kept finding more clothes to try on.

Most naked women I see are in locker rooms at swimming pools or fitness classes, tugging on tights or standing under showers. Their bodies are knock-kneed or long-waisted, narrow-shouldered or broad-hipped. Striking, the differences in the length and breadth of our bones. But most of the naked women I see are toned, aloof, and tend to be touchy about the shape they're in.

In the factory I saw women whose skin flowed over their abdomens like pancake batter, puddled over their underpants like icing sagging down a warm cake onto the plate. Their faces didn't warn me. They stood and walked normally, spoke with humour, unzipped each other. *I'll buy it, but I want to lose seven pounds.*

One woman's legs had no muscle; the bones of her thighs wore a summer jacket of flesh, but her stomach had slipped from under her bra and belled out in an exaggerated lip that rolled over her hips. She was cheerful and chatty, energetic. She asked me if the pants she was trying on were too baggy in the bum. *Could you take them in a bit?* I suggest.

It's dim in the warehouse and there are only a few mirrors leaning against the walls. I feel guilty about going shopping. It takes too much time. I have enough clothes. The grey suit's classy, but boring. Why am I spending money? I should be at the computer.

My ego roles had a tantrum when I left them at home. I can hear them hiccup and whimper. It's like needing to nurse a baby and your breasts starting to leak, just from remembering her. I sat in a bar years ago streaming milk, determined to have one beer with my husband, covering my front with my coat, feeling the wet dress cling all the way to my waist. The milk spilling, soaking into my panties – I held my coat out from my body so it wouldn't get stained. That's how it is – there's scant gain, it seems, in not doing what people need me to do, when they need it.

I'm not sure what I'm supposed to learn from one unusual afternoon. Especially since, as usual, I've been trying to do the right thing. Grandmother Spider, the book said, gives unimpressive but essential wisdom. The clothes were a bargain. Good for teaching. But the naked women are the real prize. Seeing run-of-the-mill bodies undressed. Why was I surprised? At my age? How closeted we are. After all our reading and meetings and tirades. Remember Rembrandt? He knew.

A wardrobe of grey wool – trousseau of invisibility. Grandmother Spider's uniform. I expect more.

Maxie's Wake

Standing about in her front room.
Two bed sheets of light
– neat ironed squares –
hung on the walls opposite
the mullioned beach window
and the east window.

Sunshine gone to cotton
without her conversation.
Squares and sandwiches. Champagne.
Grieving in a grey suit with a purple belt.
Drinking enough to feel it.

Maxie
gave things away
if she hadn't used them in two years.
Slept under a rosary. Said the nuns
in their grey habits
taught her the art of flirting.
Divorced at twenty-three in Vienna,
she went with her father, a surgeon, to China.
In Shanghai, married my uncle,
who stood six-foot four and
rode horseback across Mongolia.
With a baby, escaping a revolution,
came by sea to Canada. In a logging camp,
lived for the first time without servants.
Preferred a pebble beach,
sitting on the floor, a smaller fire.
Took her son to Austria; again, war broke out.
Walked across the Alps,
then sailed back to the coast.
Taxed her heart daily,
swam in the ocean May through September.
Selected friends carefully.

Liked Buddhists.
Charmed people by choice.
Loved, until their deaths,
her husband with Parkinson's
and an Englishman who kept her garden.
'The best years for a woman,' she said,
'are those between forty and sixty.'
The last time she let me see her,
Maxie and I sat,
each with a gin and tonic, under her patio umbrella
as she explained
'Life is not worth living without love,'
that I must have her clothes, and
how she'd organized her death.
'The doctors spoke of an operation
but I said no.'
Waves tame and distant. She reached over and rearranged
the florist's pink roses.
'Jane,' she said,
'I have adored my life.'

Bordering her white
shack, as she called it, meticulous
blue bells, poppies, lavender clumps.
Ocean beyond the rockery
and Maxie slender, ironic, stretched out
with a book in her hand and the sun in her face.

Salt Woman

salt
rim to a small lake, a mere
she called it, leftover from a previous life
salt woman on the verge
savoring herself

sal sapienta
sharpened by evaporation
a little salt makes sugar sweeter
and lemon tangy
white crust

salt
cleans a wound smartly
rough crystal
common as the first name you share with thousands
yet recognize as your own

salt
brings out the flavour
does not fester

Shelburne Farms

Jazz, the golden lab, gallops behind us,
keeps pace: twenty m.p.h., passes the car,
lopes from side to side of the dirt road,
tongue flapping, hind feet crossing fore feet.

Vermont hills in October, sumac
licking through bronzed maples, and Jazz
racing into the grass: hips, haunches,
his ears turned inside out, tail unbuckled.

At the market garden, chickens:
ten-week-old meat birds. Slaughter date set.
In the shed, sacks of potatoes.
Finger-thick willow whips in a cane-brake
between fields. Baskets on the front porch.

The land's hand rests on Lake Champlain. Jazz swims
into whitecaps. Gulls turn on falling
edges of air as the afternoon incorporates rain.
Above the ridge a handful of birds, tossed
up and back into the trees. From the north,
geese: long necks, flap of wings like wet sails.

Jazz bounds around the cows whose ears
tip towards me, brown ears
peaked and lined with white hair.
Cows' eyes round as deers'. The herd
draws close, listening
to compliments: *you beautiful creatures,*
exquisite beasts. Eight deer
in a higher meadow. We follow paths and the road,
Jazz racing ahead, looping variations on our walk.

When We Lived On West Tenth

the clap of footsteps down wooden stairs
the breakfast orange peeled and segmented
a gargoyle above the kitchen window
messages on the chalkboard
dust on the computer
a rose atop the clock radio
dinner by candlelight within the fist of winter
black cat fur on the white chair
emptying the compost bucket
a drawing of orchids in my study
an open drawer of cassettes, his boxes of records
a ring of crocus on the back grass
peas along the fence, greens in raised beds
turning the futon on Sunday
a small mirror in the big bathroom
a shell from Mahabalipuram
the phone's memory
bed, wonderful bed
books piled on both sides
hand in hand at midnight
Monk's music in the air

Anon

days in the rain
energy to be explained
resolving the ultraviolet catastrophe
planck, plinck, plonk
quanta drum on the gutter
and way out at sea
amidst paradoxes and possibilities
a mermaid is a mathematical trick
I am egg and sperm
oh, my wiggly tail, sweet smile,
black body curve
as the pacific oscillates
pours down the coast, oh, mountains
on my side, love
in my arms again

The Fine Minutiae Of Moments

for my mother

The apple tree held back its bloom this year.

Recalling the way you'd say, *Janie – come and see,*
I find you outside in the rain: apron,
flip-flops, grey hair in a bun, face aglow,
pointing up at the yellow transparent
in its delicate array behind our log house.

Today, it's as if this city tree
planned to flower on your birthday, the way
Easter arrived when you turned five,
the cat had kittens, the sow piglets,
the orchard blossomed, and you, lit up with measles
had to miss it all.

Remembering your birthday, I remember your death.
Snip a twig: two crimson buds, a handful of petals.
You welcomed posies: nosegays of clover,
fireweed in a tumbler on the windowsill.

Whenever I put a bouquet in the kitchen
you cross my mind. Our recent pink tulips
lasted a week. This morning their flaps hang down,
one already on the counter.

Pink. Pink. Pink.
Your charred skin. The black month
you wrestled death.

Janie – come and see, you beckon
in your green dress with the white belt,
you hold up soup bones from the butcher,
roll the ball of a thigh in its hip socket
to illustrate articulation.

Even in the hospital
with half your skin burned away
you observed yourself learning, told me
Simplicity is more and more difficult.

The brass Buddha
the size of a large cat,
the weight of a big dictionary,
melted in the fire. I found his right foot
and folded hands, attached to the wrinkles
of his torso, dropped like a shirt
on the ash and cinders. All grey now.
Sometimes I rub the palm of his foot.

I in you and you in I
go back through the placenta.
Before lungs, before the crunchy lightness
of bones, through the memory of a cell.
Your mother is also in my mind.
And still there are the fine minutiae
of moments. Our own. The particulars.
An apple orchard in bloom when you turned five.
Your yellow transparent beside the huckleberry bush.
The amber bellies of logs
reflecting light in a log house.
You I grew inside of.

23, 20, 19

my children
gone, and not gone, tidal

my hands
having handled the world for them
rest a moment on their shoulders
hold till I feel their muscles adjust
to balance its weight

but sometimes, a child comes to me again
then, whatever I may be full of
I set aside
to hold still that ocean
in which a child rounds true to self
in my hands

Hyacinth

Basting the faces together, just to try this place
on for size. Basting stitches. Basting in my own fat,
that's what. The best place here's the coffee shop.
All the pretty girls don't have kids at home,
and the grey-haired, super-natural women scare me.
They've thought about too much. It shows
in their choice of shoes. My shoulder hurts –
this bag's too heavy. In the registrar's office they
told me *You've got all deficiencies!*
No grade point average. No math. No science.
No foreign language. No English composition.
No employer's name. No spouse to speak of.

And no softness in my voice.
That cuticle's bleeding again.
They're polite, but no one has the slightest idea
of the mess in the kitchen or the kid with bronchitis.
What did she mean, *reentry woman!*
I never had the chance to be here before.
Women's work turned to the inside.
Blind hems. Hidden seams. Who counts the stitches
it takes to make a deficient life?
One that doesn't fit anymore.

Mama left me grandma's gold thimble.
Good women, daughters of farm women,
raised in the church. At sixteen, grandma
put up her hair and wore long skirts.
At sixteen, mama embroidered linens.
At sixteen, I failed math and made that green dress.
My farm's the window sill. By the time I was nineteen,
I had a daughter, and a husband. There's been plenty
of growing-up around me. *Deficiencies!* Maybe.
But raising kids gives you persistence.

Last night, I heard the hyacinth crack its plastic pot.
A root clawed through the green shell.
No needle. No thimble. Just that thread.
Ate a peep-hole, then let her rip – the coiled growth
from inside straightening out, nosing into space.
Tree roots heave paved roads.
Seed leaves lift pebbles.
Morning-glory rises through
cement step, baseboard, window frame.
Climbs summer long inside the front hall.

All deficiencies? Reentry?
The force that drives a hyacinth root
comes from the years it bloomed and sank.
Just because you're vulnerable
doesn't mean you're weak.
Mama would push me into this, if she could.
Perhaps that's reentry – generations
packed into my head and heart,
a full bulb, freshly planted.

Fishing Sonnet

Eating perfectly sauced red snapper, curled improbably in
boneless rosettes

instead of waiting for dusk, rowing along the cliff, trolling a
line until it tenses, yanks heavy.

You've been out there day after day, trailing your pole,
burning in the sun, idling, shifting, paddling along.

You cast, dawdle, jig – diddle the layers of deep water

in which things invisible live: your flimsy line, the plump
seals, the canny finned flock

– but, this evening, a hidden fish pulls on your wrists,

its struggle echoes in your belly. Rod bowed, one end wedged
against your hip, the other scribbling across the lip of air
pulled back from bare water,

and then: so alive: the quick flipping body

twitching – flopping over aluminium frets across the bottom
of the boat, at your feet

as you catch another. Another. Five red snappers. Mouths
sucking air. Club each fish but it slips, jumps again.

Chill as you rip the cord to start the motor. Noise. Noise.
And the beach boulders bang, your shoes and cuffs soaked

in the cold water. Clean them fast. Slit, scrape, the bloody
back bones still alive. Fish nerves. You know someone with
such nerve. Almost, the fillets leap.

Cook them by lantern light.

Swallow sweet greenish flesh tinged with slaughter, your
throat too tense for talk.

It's In The Kitchen

mostly I hear music
while we're eating dinner
or fixing food
all the sensual pleasures
towards the end of day
set my hips to circling
fingertips converting
knife riffs to a backbeat
how the final measure drops right off

now if I could counterpoint
here amidst the line
some fancy sister's pyrotechnics
you'd listen to the melody's sequins swing
and then that long wry stabbed-heart plea
she sings – a good man, she claims
is hard
to find

coming or going
she's got a handy man, handy
with the stride
of opposites
his left hand, sometimes slighted, stomping there
rocks across two octaves
lifts a saxophone elegy, its full hunger
love, she sings again, is a child believing
oom-pah below the tinkling
picked bones shimmy

we're cooking in the kitchen
garlic smoking
slicing zukes and cukes, mixing
me, myself and I licked off a finger
leaves above the eaves, and a child out in the garden
singing the blues and crying
where peaches hang like globes of honey
along branches of an orchard in a darkened heaven
plums, gleaming like aubergines
become the jam of this year's kisses
to have found your place on earth
no, no, they can't take that away from me

deep rhythm captivates me
it's not just the tension
of swing, curve of a horn
deep in the centre of jazz as it's sounding
its sweet confirmation
we're human, honey
swaying and cooking
regrets syncopated – it's that little delay
without your love
that's not quite safe
lordy, how it wrinkles the mind
we're funny that way

In The Time Of The Dying Of Mothers

The black cat has crept up to lie between our waists. I am not sleeping and feel her warm against my hip. She is licking her paws, between the claws. I can tell by the way her back shifts and the snuffling noises she makes. She has lived with you longer than I have. Billie, because she is black and she is beautiful.

Mink, mother's Burmese, and earlier, Tillie, Mink's tabby mother – and before Tillie, Apricat, the apricot-point Siamese, and Kimchi, the loutish Siamese, and Tiny, the huge Persian – generations of cats – mother's shadows as she moved through the house. Standing at the mahogany counter, cutting raw liver on an arborite square, talking baby-talk to Mink who is stretching her neck to rub it against mother's shins. If Mink had not died earlier that year she would have caught the pack-rat who chewed the insulation and shorted the wires. The fire would not have started. My mother might still be alive.

A duster in hand. Pensively, shaking it out, out a casement window. So many gestures. Memories. Sifting flour onto a sheet of wax paper. Refolding the paper in quarters. Leaving it in the sifter.

A smooth rock that fits into my palm. Walking on the beach at Boundary Bay, mother hands me flat stones – smooth stones. I keep the softest oval. My soft stone. Smooth as skin, but cool.

Thick skins, broken, piled on the kitchen table. Oil of oranges in the air after breakfast.

I do not have another mother. My aunts have died. Even my mother-in-law.

Lilacs by the driveway. African violet on the table. Homemade oat cakes cut in triangles. Silver knives rolled in red flannel. White porcelain sink on its pedestal. Head over the sink as she poured vinegar through my hair. Scent and smart of vinegar. Rinsing dark hair till it squeaked.

Windbreak of poplars around a farm yard. Walking to visit a woman who had wicker furniture in her front room. Sitting on the floor in a sunny corner while mother talked. Playing with buttons. Buttons from a round tin with a painted plaid ribbon. The delta cut up now, trees felled, stumps bulldozed, its deep ditches filled in. Ditches where people drowned each year, gone. Potato fields gone to houses. Blueberries torn up. Malls. Garden condominiums. Three college campuses. Highways. The buttons seemed to be mine – mother's friend lifted the tin down for me each time.

Pins in her mouth when she sewed. Pinned up a hem. Pursing her lips, repinning, as I turned slowly. A friend showed me a dress her mother made for her, just a few years ago. Spreading it out on the bed, smoothing an arm under it to show me the print. The drift of cotton over skin. Our mothers made us many dresses. Outfitted us.

It is as if here, in the middle of life, I have wandered into a deep forest. Musty, fungus-laden spars criss-cross a bog where my feet sink unevenly and no log is solid for its full length. I dream of refugees.

When I stop sleeping there is our body warmth, the breathing, a nest on the surface of the dark. This can't be the desert of the mystics because love keeps me company and the black cat has come in the window.

Through my enchantment of grief, mother's sharp whistle: two fingers under her tongue – *come home now, come home.*

There is no place like home. Come home, spirit, knocking on doors, out on the streets in your slip.

Acknowledgements

Some of these poems first appeared in *Canadian Literature, The Capilano Review, Event, The Malahat Review, Poetry Canada Review, Quarry, Prism international, The Canadian Journal for the Study of Adult Education,* and *Proceedings of* AERC *(1987, 88, 92)*.

Some were broadcast on CO-OP Radio's 'radio free rainforest' programme.

'Hyacinth' was commissioned by Linda Lewis for a book entitled *Addressing the Needs of Returning Women,* San Francisco: Jossey-Bass Inc., 1988.

I am grateful for financial assistance from The Canada Council and to family and friends for their encouragement and support. In particular, I want to thank Jan Zwicky and also Roo Borson, Kim Maltman, Don McKay, Sharon Thesen, Jan Conn, and my husband, Bob Amussen, for their perceptive reading, editorial insights and good advice.

About the Author

Jane Southwell Munro grew up and raised a family in Vancouver. The author of two previous collections of poetry, *Daughters* and *The Trees Just Moved Into A Season Of Other Shapes*, she has travelled widely in Europe and Asia, holds a doctorate in Adult Education, has taught at The University of British Columbia, and now teaches Creative Writing at Kwantlen University College. She lives with her husband in a house in the woods on the west coast of Vancouver Island.

PENNY STREET